HOW ALASKA GOT ITS FLAG

by

Bernd and Susan Richter

Published by

Saddle Pal Creations, Inc., Wasilla, Alaska, USA

Acknowledgements:
We are grateful to the following for assisting us with this book project:
The University of Alaska Foundation for granting permission to use the Alaska
flag song; Patti Green, Stu Schulman, and the McDonald family and trust for
authorizing the use of Michael McDonald's rendition of the Alaska flag song;
Kurt Riehman of Surreal Studios for advice and expertise; and Linda Thurston
for her editing efforts.

> **To Don Newman and Mary K. McDonald**

Text and illustration copyright © 2000 by Bernd and Susan Richter
Printed in China; Second Edition, Second Printing, January 2009
ISBN-10: 1-931353-22-0; ISBN-13: 978-1-931353-22-9;
Designed, produced, published, and distributed in Alaska by:
   Bernd and Susan Richter
   Saddle Pal Creations, Inc., P.O. Box 872127, Wasilla, AK 99687, USA

More children's books by Bernd and Susan Richter available from Saddle Pal Creations, Inc.:

* When Grandma and Grandpa visited Alaska they ...
* Grandma and Grandpa Visit Denali Natl. Park
* Grandma and Grandpa Cruise Alaska's Inside Passage
* Grandma and Grandpa Ride the Alaska Train
* When G'ma and G'pa Rode the White Pass (board b.)
* When G'ma and G'pa Cruised through Alaska (board b.)
* When G'ma and G'pa Rode the Alaska Train (board b.)
* Alaska Animals - Where do they go at 40 below?
* The Little Bear Who Didn't Want to Hibernate
* Uncover Alaska's Wonders (a lift-the-flap book)
* Good Morning Alaska - Good Morning Little Bear (board)
* Goodnight Alaska - Goodnight Little Bear (board book)
* Peek-A-Boo Alaska (lift-the-flap board book)
* How Animal Moms Love Their Babies (board book)
* Touch and Feel Alaska's Animals (board book)

* How Alaska Got Its Flag
* There Was A Little Bear
* There Was A Little Porcupine
* I See You Through My Heart
* Do Alaskans Live in Igloos?
* Cruising Alaska's Inside Passage
* Listen to Alaska's Animals (sound book)
* She's My Mommy Too!
* My Alaska Animals - Can You name Them?
* The Twelve Days of Christmas in Alaska
* Discover Alaska's Denali park
* A Bus Ride Into Denali (board book)
* When Grandma visited Alaska she ...
* Old Maid - Alaska Style (card game)
.... and more

Look at these books by visiting our website **www.alaskachildrensbooks.com**

Introduction

This is the story of young Benny Benson,
an Alaska Aleut Native.
Many years ago, at the very early age of 13 years,
Benny's name appeared on the front page of
newspapers all over the United States.
Even today, Benny is well remembered
in Alaska where streets and schools are
named after him.
Why was his name in the newspapers?
What was it that made him so famous in Alaska
for all time to come?
Continue reading and you will find out.
Enjoy!

Join us on a journey back in time, all the way to the year 1926. At that time, the United States of America consisted of 48 states (not 50, like today) and 2 territories, Alaska and Hawaii. During official ceremonies, 49 flags represented the 48 states and two territories. Are you wondering why there were only 49 flags? Obviously, something was wrong. Did one state have two flags? Was there a law that territories couldn't have their own flag? The truth is much simpler. The territory of Alaska, by far the largest of all the states and territories, didn't have a flag at all. This bothered the governor of Alaska George A. Parks so much that he finally decided in 1926 that Alaska should have its own flag. This was 60 years after Alaska had become a territory of the United States.

Governor Parks knew that Alaskans wanted the very best design for their flag. He could have asked a professional flag maker to come up with a design. Instead, the decision was made to have a contest among young Alaskan students to assure that a variety of ideas and designs from the entire territory would be considered for Alaska's own flag.

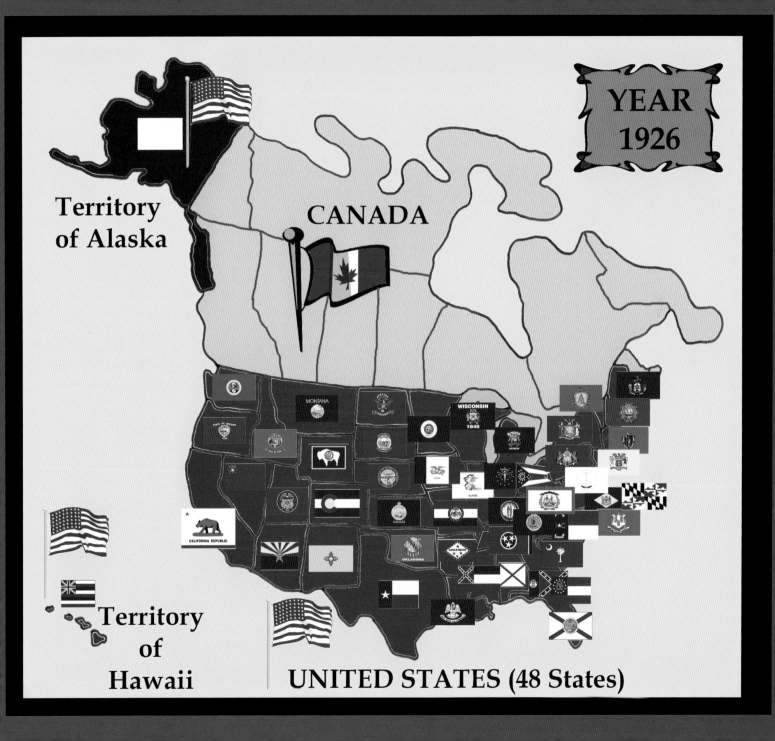

Teachers all over Alaska announced to their excited students that "The design contest is open to all of Alaska's schoolchildren seventh grade and up."

"What is there to win?" students asked with great anticipation. The teachers explained, "The winner of the contest will receive a beautiful gold pocket watch. Those in second and third places will win fine cash prices. Most importantly, being the winner would be an incredible accomplishment for which you could be very proud. Also, the winner will become famous all over Alaska because the winning design will be made into a flag that will represent Alaska forever!"

There was a loud commotion in all the classrooms, as children were yelling out their ideas and what would be good and what wouldn't. "Hold on, hold on," the teachers said. "There's plenty of time for you to think about design ideas later. Go home now, put your ideas down on paper, and then let's see what we like best and what we will send on to the judges in our capital city of Juneau."

Benny Benson was a 7th grade student at Seward's Jesse Lee Mission School at that time. "How lucky I'm not in 6th grade," he thought on his way home from school. "This way I can be part of this historical contest. Winning won't be easy," he concluded. "There will be so many kids trying for the prizes."

Benny already had lots of ideas floating in his head. Even though he was still quite young, Benny knew Alaska very well as he had spent a lot of time outdoors fishing with his father, hunting with his uncle, and gathering berries with his mother. He had seen the riches of Alaska: the oceans with their whales, walrus and seals; the mighty land animals, such as grizzly bears and moose; and he had explored the forests and mountains that surround his home. Benny also had read a lot about things he hadn't seen yet - the caribou herds with tens of thousands of animals, the salmon runs that count in the hundreds of thousands, and the rich gold mines worth millions and millions of dollars.

"Alaska is full of special things and places," he thought. By the time he reached his home, Benny had decided that Alaska's flag should reflect all of these wonderful things.

Back in his room, Benny was anxious to put some of his ideas on paper. Right after he finished his homework, he took some drawing paper and colored pencils out of his desk drawer and started to draw. He drew the designs on paper as quickly as the ideas came into his head. Oh, what fun he had! Soon, the entire table was covered with sheets of drawing paper. When he ran out of space on the table, he put the designs on his bed. After a few hours, there wasn't enough room on his bed anymore, and he began spreading them out on the floor. He hoped nobody would come and see the mess he had made. "Phew!" Benny sighed, after he had drawn for several hours. When he looked at all of his pictures, he murmered to himself, "There are way too many designs. The teacher and the judges won't have the time to look at all these pictures. I'd better sort them and pick out the very best."

Benny liked all of his designs, and it was very difficult for him to decide which ones to keep and which ones to discard. Yet, he knew that he would have to narrow his choices because only the best one would have a chance to win. That evening he chose his nine favorite pictures:

(1) Mt. McKinley, the highest mountain in Alaska and all of North America;

(2) Snowflakes, which reminded him of Christmas and Alaska's long winters;

(3) A caribou, an important food source for many people in Alaska;

(4) The trees, which provide wood for houses and for heating in the winter;

(5) The outline of the territory of Alaska;

(6) The mighty grizzly bear, like the one his uncle brought home from a summer hunt;

(7) The miner, looking for gold in Alaska's rivers;

(8) The coastline, the part of Alaska that was settled first and where he was born; and

(9) The flowers, which cover Alaska so beautifully each summer.

"That will do for today," Benny said to himself as he got ready for bed.

Alaska *Alaska*

AK

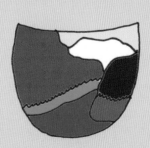

Alaska

That night Benny dreamed of flags and more flags. Strangely enough, in the middle of one of those dreams, he suddenly saw a picture of himself and his mother. They were standing at the coast, waiting for his father to come home from a fishing trip. It was late at night, and the sky was full of stars.

"How will Papa find his way home in the dark, Mom?" a worried Benny asked.

"Don't you worry," his mother replied gently. "The stars will show your Papa the way home. You see, Papa is an experienced fisherman who knows the stars very well. He knows all the constellations and can even tell you the names of individual stars. Do you see the seven stars that look like a giant dipper? This constellation is called the 'Big Dipper'. There's also a 'Little Dipper', which includes a very important star, called the North Star. You find the North Star at the end of the handle of the 'Little Dipper' and in a direct line with the two end stars on the scoop part of the 'Big Dipper'. The North Star indicates the north direction. By knowing the stars and by knowing where the stars are in relation to our little cove, your Papa always finds his way home."

When Benny woke up the next morning, he went straight to his desk to look at his designs again. No matter which picture he looked at, his mind was with last night's dream and its sparkling stars in the night sky. Almost without thinking, he took some more sheets of paper from his drawer and began to draw stars. First, he drew one big star right in the center of the page. Then he tried another picture with lots and lots of stars. Finally, he remembered the Big Dipper and drew its seven stars. Benny then added the North Star and colored all those stars with the brightest gold he could find. He liked this design, but he wanted those stars to look even brighter. So he took a dark and very pretty blue and filled the paper with it, carefully drawing around the golden stars.

"I like it," he shouted with excitement when he was done. "No, I don't just like it. I love it! This is the best design of all! This is the one I will submit for the contest." After he had admired his design for awhile, he sat down and wrote the following words under it, so the judges would understand the meaning of his design:

The blue field is for the Alaska sky and the forget-me-not, an Alaskan flower. The North Star is for the future of the state of Alaska, the most northerly in the Union. The Dipper is for the Great Bear, symbolizing strength.
(Benny Benson, Seward, Alaska, 1926)

When it was time to submit the designs, Benny stood in line with all of the other children of his class and the higher classes at his school. The seventh graders, including Benny, were very worried that the older boys and girls might have an advantage because the older students had already learned so much more than they had. However, everybody's design was accepted, and everybody's name was recorded together with the entry. Fifty designs were submitted that day, which was way too many to forward to the judges from a single school. So all of the teachers got together to pick the seven best designs. Benny's design came in third. This wasn't bad, but Benny had hoped for a better outcome. "Oh well," Benny thought, "it doesn't really matter which place the teachers gave me. The important thing is that I made it to the final. The real judging will be done by the judges in Juneau, and they may still vote for me."

Out of several hundred entries by students from all over Alaska teachers selected and submitted still more than 100 entries for the final judging. Each and every one of these entries was considered good enough to be the possible winner. Now that's competition!

It wasn't easy for the judges to make their selection. They compared and went over the pictures again and again. They were very careful because their final decision would be of historical importance.

Finally, after many hours, each judge made a decision and wrote on note cards his or her first, second, and third choices. It was time for the judges to compare notes and choose the winner of the flag design contest. At a given signal, the judges went to their No. 1, No. 2, and No. 3 choices to post their note cards on their favorite designs.

What a surprise! They all agreed!

Each and every one of the judges had given the design by Benny Benson the top honor. There was no question that Benny's design of eight stars on a dark blue background was the winner and would be the future flag of Alaska. The judges were happy that they all had chosen the same design, and they were proud of Alaska's beautiful new flag.

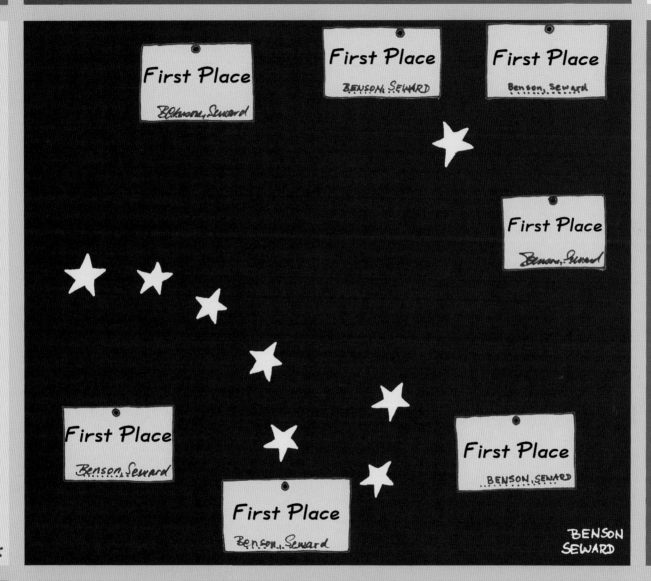

When news of Benny's victory reached the school, the excitement was too much to be contained. The teacher was so happy for young Benny that she broke out in tears. Benny's classmates stood on the tables cheering, "Benny, Benny, our hero." They would slap him on the shoulders; shake hands to congratulate him; dance around the tables; run up and down the hallways yelling, "Benny won, Benny won," and behave in a way that normally would have gotten them into big trouble. But it was a special day and the school principal didn't mind. It was such an honor for this little school in Seward to have in its ranks the winner of a territory-wide contest that the principal declared the day a holiday for the entire school. "Let's celebrate and go home early," he announced. This, of course, made the students cheer even more. Only Benny sat quietly on his chair as the rest celebrated. Like his teacher, he was overwhelmed by what had happened. He didn't cry, but he was speechless. He couldn't quite believe that the dream of winning had come true for him.

But, true it was!

The next day, there was a big headline in the local newspaper, announcing to everybody that Benny Benson had won the flag-design contest. It was official, and everybody could read about it. There was even a picture of Benny and his flag design on the front page. As if that wasn't enough, an official delegation from the government in Juneau came to Seward to congratulate Benny and to present him with his gold pocket watch. It was a great day for Benny and for the little town of Seward!

Not only was it a great day for Benny but for all Alaskans as well. Alaska now had its own place among all the other flags of the states and territories of the United States of America. Many still consider Benny's flag one of the prettiest in the nation. Do you agree? If not, which of the flags do you like best? If you could participate in a flag contest for your town, state, or country, how would your flag look?

THE END (almost)

A few years after Benny's design had been officially declared Alaska's flag, Marie Drake wrote a poem about the flag and Elinor Dusenbury composed piano music to that poem. Alaskans liked the poem and the music so much that they made them the offical Alaska flag song. Turn the page to read the poem. You can listen to a beautiful version of the Alaska flag song performed by Michael K. McDonald, also known as "Sourdough Mike", on the CD attached to the inside back cover of this book. Enjoy!

 ALABAMA

 ARIZONA

 ARKANSAS

 CALIFORNIA

 COLORADO

 CONNECTICUT

 DELAWARE

 FLORIDA

 GEORGIA

 HAWAII

 IDAHO

 ILLINOIS

 INDIANA

 IOWA

 KANSAS

 KENTUCKY

 LOUISIANA

 MAINE

 MARYLAND

 MASSACHUSETTS

 MICHIGAN

 MINNESOTA

 MISSISSIPPI

 MISSOURI

 MONTANA

 NEBRASKA

 NEVADA

 ALASKA

 NEW HAMPSHIRE

 NEW JERSEY

 NEW MEXICO

 NEW YORK

 NORTH CAROLINA

 NORTH DAKOTA

 OHIO

 OKLAHOMA

 OREGON

 PENNSYLVANIA

 RHODE ISLAND

SOUTH CAROLINA

 SOUTH DAKOTA

 TENNESSEE

 TEXAS

 UTAH

 VERMONT

VIRGINIA

WASHINGTON

WEST VIRGINIA

WISCONSIN

WYOMING

Alaska Flag Song

(words by Marie Drake, 1935)

Eight stars of gold on a field of blue,
Alaska's flag, may it mean to you,
The blue of the sea, the evening sky,
The mountain lakes and the flowers nearby,
The gold of the early sourdough's dreams,
The precious gold of the hills and streams,
The brilliant stars in the northern sky,
The "Bear," the "Dipper," and shining high,
The great North Star with its steady light,
O'er land and sea a beacon bright,
Alaska's flag to Alaskans dear,
The simple flag of the last frontier.

ALASKA

More Children's Books by Bernd and Susan Richter

Saddle Pal Creations, P.O. Box 872127, Wasilla, AK 99687; www.alaskachildrensbooks.com

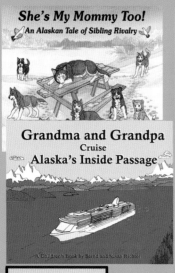

She's My Mommy Too!
An Alaskan Tale of Sibling Rivalry

Grandma and Grandpa
Cruise
Alaska's Inside Passage

A Children's Book by Bernd and Susan Richter

The Little Bear Who
Didn't Want To
Hibernate
or
Even Bear Moms Know Best

A Children's Tale by Bernd & Susan Richter
Illustrated by Sue Green

I See You
Through
My
Heart

by Diane & Donna Drashner and Bernd & Susan Richter
Illustrations by Diane Drashner and Bernd Richter

Old Maid
Alaska Style

**Old Maid -
card game**

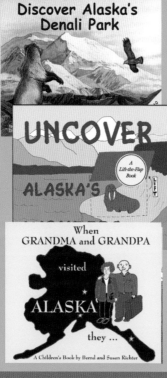

**Discover Alaska's
Denali Park**

**UNCOVER
ALASKA'S**
A Lift-the-Flap Book

When
GRANDMA and GRANDPA
visited
ALASKA
they ...

A Children's Book by Bernd and Susan Richter

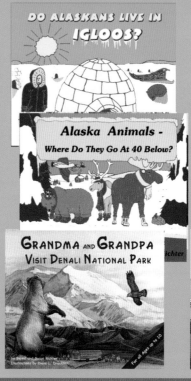

DO ALASKANS LIVE IN IGLOOS?

**Alaska Animals -
Where Do They Go At 40 Below?**

GRANDMA and **GRANDPA**
VISIT DENALI NATIONAL PARK

by Bernd and Susan Richter
Illustrations by Diane L. Drashner

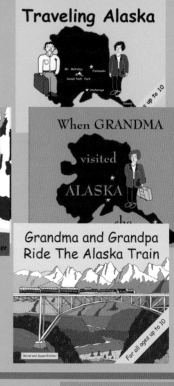

Traveling Alaska

When GRANDMA
visited
ALASKA

**Grandma and Grandpa
Ride The Alaska Train**

Bernd and Susan Richter

For all ages up to 10

Board Books

THERE WAS
A LITTLE
PORCUPINE

An Alaskan Tale
by
Bernd & Susan Richter
Illustrations by Diane Drashner & Bernd Richter

THERE WAS
A LITTLE
BEAR

An Alaskan Tale by
Bernd & Susan Richter
Illustrations by Diane Drashner & Bernd Richter

When
Grandma and Grandpa
visited
Alaska
they ...
A Children's Book by Bernd and Susan Richter
For all Ages up to 4

When
Grandma and Grandpa
Cruised
Through Alaska . . .
A Children's Book by Bernd and
Ages 0 to 4

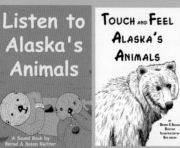

**Listen to
Alaska's
Animals**

A Sound Book by
Bernd and Susan Richter

**TOUCH and FEEL
ALASKA'S
ANIMALS**

BY
BERND & SUSAN
RICHTER
ILLUSTRATED BY
SUE GREEN

**Peek-A-Boo
Alaska**
A Lift-the-Flap Book

by Bernd and Susan Richter

**Goodnight Alaska -
Goodnight
Little Bear**

Bernd & Susan Richter

**How
Animal Moms
Love Their
Babies**

**Alaskan Toys -
For Girls and Boys**

**My Alaska Animals -
Can you
name
them?**

**A Bus Ride Into
DENALI**

by
Bernd
and
Susan
Richter

"Alaska's Flag"
performed by Michael K. McDonald and
recorded on CD "Sourdough Mike's Favorite Songs."
Used with permission of copyright holder; copyright © 2000 McDonald Music.
Recorded at Mountain View 48 Track Digital, Anchorage,
and Surreal Studios, Anchorage, Alaska.
Produced and arranged by Stu Schulman and Mike McDonald.
Engineered by Kurt Riehman; assisted by Kristi Olson.